Who Was King Tut?

Claire Dormant

Who Was King Tut?

By Roberta Edwards
Illustrated by True Kelley

Grosset & Dunlap

For Judy Donnelly—R.E.

For Charlotte and Eloise Lindblom—T.K.

GROSSET & DUNLAP
Published by the Penguin Group
Penguin Group (USA) Inc., 375 Hudson Street, New York, New York 10014, USA
Penguin Group (Canada), 90 Eglinton Avenue East, Suite 700,
Toronto, Ontario M4P 2Y3, Canada (a division of Pearson Penguin Canada Inc.)
Penguin Books Ltd., 80 Strand, London WC2R 0RL, England
Penguin Group Ireland, 25 St. Stephen's Green, Dublin 2, Ireland
(a division of Penguin Books Ltd.)
Penguin Group (Australia), 250 Camberwell Road, Camberwell, Victoria 3124, Australia
(a division of Pearson Australia Group Pty. Ltd.)
Penguin Books India Pvt. Ltd., 11 Community Centre,
Panchsheel Park, New Delhi—110 017, India
Penguin Group (NZ), 67 Apollo Drive, Rosedale, Auckland 0632, New Zealand
(a division of Pearson New Zealand Ltd.)
Penguin Books (South Africa) (Pty.) Ltd., 24 Sturdee Avenue,
Rosebank, Johannesburg 2196, South Africa

Penguin Books Ltd., Registered Offices: 80 Strand, London WC2R 0RL, England

Text copyright © 2006 by Penguin Group (USA) Inc. Illustrations copyright © 2006 by
True Kelley. Cover illustration copyright © 2006 by Nancy Harrison. All rights reserved.
Published by Grosset & Dunlap, a division of Penguin Young Readers Group,
345 Hudson Street, New York, New York 10014. GROSSET & DUNLAP is a trademark
of Penguin Group (USA) Inc. Printed in the U.S.A.

Library of Congress Control Number: 2005025504

ISBN 978-0-448-44360-7 (pbk)
ISBN 978-0-448-46677-4 (HC)

33 32 31
10 9 8 7 6 5 4 3 2 1

Contents

Contents

Who Was
King Tut?

In June of 2005, pharaoh fever struck California. In just one month, half a million people streamed into the Los Angeles County Museum of Art. They wanted to see the dazzling jewelry and household items that once belonged to a king of Egypt.

Everyone was very excited to see beautiful furniture and lamps, musical instruments, and board games. So many people came, the museum had to stay open until eleven o'clock at night.

There was a small chair the king used as a child. There was a chariot that he used to ride. There was a couch in the shape

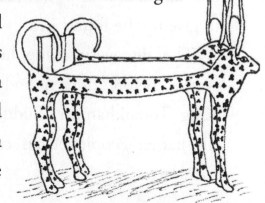

of two spotted cows. Objects that had once belonged to other pharaohs were also on display. There were about one hundred and twenty-five objects, including fans and vases and folding chairs and clothes.

Although many things looked brand-new, they weren't. They were more than three thousand years old. For all that time, everything lay hidden under the sands of Egypt in a secret tomb.

Early in the twentieth century, a man named Howard Carter spent years searching for the tomb. He knew the king's name: Tutankhamun. And he thought he knew where the king was buried. Finally, in 1922, just when he was about to give up, he found it.

The discovery made headlines all over the world. Before this, nobody had ever heard of King Tutankhamun. Suddenly, everyone knew his name. People began calling him King Tut for short.

Today, King Tut is probably the most famous of all the pharaohs. Yet he was not an important or powerful ruler. He was pharaoh for only about nine years. We know he got married. However, we do not even know whether he had children.

Tut died very young—when he was eighteen or nineteen years old. And the reason he died remains a mystery. Some historians think he may have been murdered.

It is strange to think that he became famous because of what was buried with him. But all the beautiful things in his tomb are important. They tell us about what life was like in ancient Egypt. And together they form a picture of who King Tut was.

Chapter 1
Gifts of the Nile

When Tut was born, around 1343 B.C., Egypt was already a very old country. Almost two thousand years old, in fact.

The Egyptian empire lay on the coast of Northern Africa, facing the Mediterranean Sea. It was a land of desert and bare hills, where the sun beat down all year long. There were few trees. And rain hardly ever came.

But the Nile River, which runs north and south, split the country in two. The Nile is the longest river in the world—a little more than four thousand miles long. It was the heart of ancient Egypt.

All along the riverbanks was rich farmland. Peasant farmers tilled their fields with plows pulled by oxen. They sprinkled seeds in the soil to grow wheat and vegetables. They raised pigs and goats and sheep. They planted fruit trees and grew grapes. The river also gave the people fish to

eat and ducks to hunt. Because of yearly flooding, there were many weeks when farmers could not work. So the river also provided "vacation" time for everyone!

The Nile was the "road" that boats traveled, bringing goods from city to city. Clay from Nile mud was used to build houses. All the great cities like Thebes and Memphis grew up near the river. Ancient Memphis may have been the first city in the world to have a million people.

From rock quarries, heavy blocks of stone were

brought on barges. They were used to build great temples and statues, some of which are still standing today.

The river was the lifeblood of the people. Without it there would have been no ancient Egypt. Just desert. But the desert was important, too. It protected Egypt. It was difficult for enemies to attack. They had to cross so many miles of sand in the blazing heat.

At one time the empire stretched from present-day Egypt south to what is now Ethiopia, east into the Sinai peninsula, and north to what is now Lebanon and Turkey.

From these other lands came ivory, furs, gold, cedar wood,

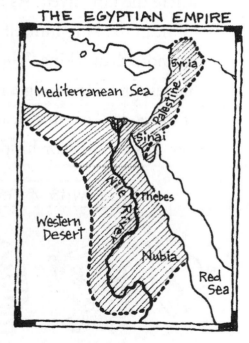

THE EGYPTIAN EMPIRE

Mediterranean Sea

Syria

Palestine

Sinai

Western Desert

Nile River

Thebes

Nubia

Red Sea

and other riches. But even as the empire grew and grew, the Egyptian way of life stayed pretty much the same. The Egyptians did not take up the customs or arts of other people. Over thousands of years, what they believed in did not change a lot, either.

For instance, their ruler was the pharaoh. The word originally meant "the great house"— where the king lived. As time went on, it came to mean the king himself. But the pharaoh was far more than a king. The pharaoh was also the highest priest and judge. He was considered a son of the gods. After his death, he became a god, too. His people worshipped him.

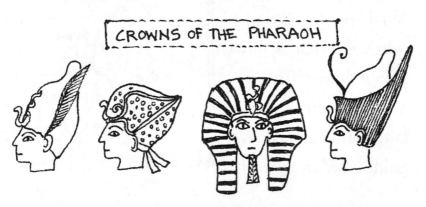

CROWNS OF THE PHARAOH

No one knows the exact day in 1343 B.C. when Tut was born. Who were his parents? Even that is not known for sure. His father was most probably Pharaoh Amenhotep IV. The pharaoh had many wives. Tut's mother may have been one of Amenhotep's less important wives.

By the time Tut was ten, he was already married. His wife was one of the pharaoh's daughters. Her name was Ankhesenamun. By this time, Tut's father had died. Tut became king. He wore the tall crowns of the pharaoh. Like all pharaohs, he wore a false beard strapped to his chin. He carried a crook and a flail (it looked like a whip). They were symbols of his power. But did he have real power? No. He was still a child.

flail

crook

false beard

Chapter 2
An Unusual Father

Of all the pharaohs who ruled Egypt, Tut's father had to be among the strangest.

First of all, there was the way he looked. Amenhotep's head was oddly shaped. It was very long and narrow. And his hips were very large for a man. Was a rare disease the cause? Some historians think so.

In spite of his looks, Amenhotep married a very beautiful queen. Two museums, one in Cairo and one in Berlin, own a bust of her. (A bust is a sculpture of someone's head and shoulders.) Her

Amenhotep

Nefertiti

name was Nefertiti. Although not of royal birth, Nefertiti looked every inch a queen.

Nefertiti became the pharaoh's head wife. Women in ancient Egypt did not have the same rights as men. For example, they did not attend school. But Nefertiti was a powerful woman. She was an important adviser to her husband.

She backed him up when he decided to make changes. Big changes.

A WOMAN PHARAOH

ALTHOUGH WOMEN IN ANCIENT EGYPT WERE NOT THE EQUALS OF MEN, IN 1504 B.C. A WOMAN BECAME PHARAOH. HER NAME WAS HATSHEPSUT. SHE TOOK POWER AFTER THE PHARAOH DIED SUDDENLY, LEAVING BEHIND ONLY ONE VERY YOUNG SON (THUTMOSE III).

MOST OF WHAT WE KNOW ABOUT HATSHEPSUT COMES FROM DEPICTIONS OF HER IN ART. AT FIRST, SHE IS SEEN IN THE TYPICAL DRESS OF A WOMAN. BUT LATER SHE IS SHOWN IN THE CROWN OF THE PHARAOH. SHE ALSO WEARS THE FALSE BEARD OF THE PHARAOH. HATSHEPSUT BEGAN MANY GREAT BUILDING PROJECTS. BUT AFTER HER DEATH AROUND 1450 B.C., THUTMOSE III BECAME PHARAOH. HE DID HIS BEST TO ERASE ANY RECORDS OF HER.

What kinds of changes did Amenhotep make?

For one thing, he decided to change the religion.

For hundreds and hundreds of years, the people of Egypt had prayed to many gods and goddesses. Some looked like people. Some looked like animals. Some had an animal head and a human body.

There was Thoth. He was the god of the moon. Anubis was the god of the cemeteries. Isis was a goddess who protected children.

Thoth

Anubis

Isis

In all, there were about a thousand different gods. Some were only local gods. But the important gods had great temples devoted to them. People could visit the temples and pray for the god's help. (Common people, however, were not allowed inside.)

Temple of Hatshepsut

The most important god of all was Amun-Ra, god of the sun. He appeared in human form. Every day he rode his chariot across the sky.

GODS AND GODDESSES

OSIRIS, ISIS, SETH, AND HORUS WERE ALSO VERY POWERFUL GODS AND GODDESSES. THESE FOUR ARE IN THE MYTH OF HOW THE EARTH AND THE UNDERWORLD BEGAN. ACCORDING TO THE MYTH, OSIRIS AND ISIS WERE KING AND QUEEN OF THE EARTH. THEY HAD A SON NAMED HORUS.

Isis   Osiris   Horus   Seth

parents → their son → his uncle

BUT OSIRIS'S BROTHER WAS JEALOUS AND WANTED TO RULE EARTH. HIS NAME WAS SETH. SO HE KILLED OSIRIS AND SENT HIM TO THE UNDERWORLD. HOWEVER, OSIRIS'S SON (HORUS) TOOK BACK THE KINGDOM FROM SETH. NOW HORUS BECAME KING OF THE EARTH. HIS FATHER, OSIRIS, BECAME KING OF THE UNDERWORLD.

SETH WAS SHOWN WITH THE HEAD OF AN IMAGINARY ANIMAL THAT LOOKS KIND OF LIKE A GREYHOUND. HE WAS GOD OF THE DESERT.

OSIRIS, GOD OF THE DEAD, WAS ALWAYS
PICTURED WRAPPED TIGHT LIKE A MUMMY.

ISIS WAS THOUGHT TO PROTECT
CHILDREN AND PEOPLE IN NEED.

HORUS HAD THE HEAD OF A
HAWK AND WAS GOD OF THE SKY.
THE EGYPTIANS BELIEVED EVERY
PHARAOH WAS THE SON OF HORUS.

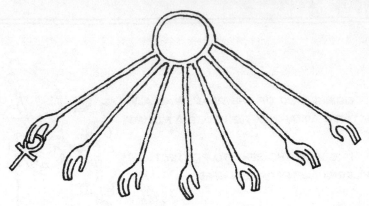

Amenhotep, however, decided to do away with all the gods and goddesses. From then on there was going to be only one god. This god was also god of the sun. But it did not appear in human form like Amun-Ra. Instead, it looked like the disk of the sun. Sun rays spread out from it. And at the end of each ray was a hand. The hands were a sign that the god was watching over the people of Egypt. The god's name was *Aten*-Ra.

The pharaoh believed he was Aten-Ra's messenger on Earth. The only way people could reach the god was through him.

Amenhotep got rid of all the priests who served other gods. Money from their temples now went to Aten-Ra. Amenhotep changed his name (to Akhenaten). His new name meant "servant of Aten." Nefertiti changed her name, too (scientists believe to Nefernefruaten). This new name meant "fair is the goddess of Aten."

The royal family moved from the city of Thebes. A new capital was built. It was called Amarna. This was where Tut spent his childhood. He grew up learning the new beliefs.

The city of Amarna spread for eight miles on either side of the Nile. Here again, Amenhotep did something different.

Usually the land west of the river was where the dead were buried. Why? Because the sun sets in the west every evening. Just as sunset brings an end to the day, death brings an end to life. So the dead were buried in the western lands. But Amenhotep decided to do the opposite in the new city. A cemetery was built east of the river. The west side of Amarna was where people lived. New homes and palaces were built as well as new temples, all to Aten-Ra.

Before this, temples had long halls that led to dark inner-rooms. This was where the priests would pray. The new temples to Aten-Ra were open-air buildings that let in the divine light of the sun.

The pharaoh also wanted to change the style of paintings. The old style had many rules for artists to follow. A person was always shown from the side. A head was always shown in profile, with one eye looking straight at the viewer. A person's face always looked young and perfect. No wrinkles or gray hair! Both shoulders always faced front, but the torso had to be shown in profile. One leg was always placed directly in front of the other. The paintings were often very beautiful, but the people in them never looked natural or three-dimensional.

Why were there so many rules for artists? The ancient Egyptians believed that a painting of a dead person could come to life. So it needed to include all the different parts of the body. An arm or a leg couldn't be left out. And the person would want to look the way he or she did when young and healthy, not when old or sick.

But Amenhotep decided to change the rules. He wanted to be portrayed as he really looked, with his long head and narrow eyes.

He also wanted paintings of people to seem more natural. Not so formal. One painting shows Amenhotep and his wife playing fondly with three of their six little daughters. Never before had anything like this been shown.

The changes, however, did not last. They were stopped soon after Amenhotep's death. (He was the pharaoh for about sixteen years.) The new city of Amarna was soon deserted. The old customs were brought back.

It must have been a very confusing time for the whole country. Just when people were getting used to all the changes, they were told to forget them. Even if Tut had already been a grown man, it would have been a difficult time to become pharaoh.

The eye of Horus wards off evil.

Chapter 3
The Boy King

Still, growing up in ancient Egypt was full of pleasures. Especially if somebody belonged to the royal famly. Tut was born a prince. He spent his childhood in a brand-new palace in Amarna.

Egyptian palaces were huge. All over the palace grounds were beautiful gardens and giant pools the

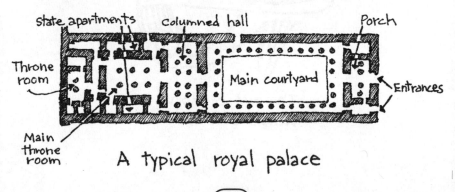

A typical royal palace

state apartments columned hall Porch

Throne room

Main courtyard

Entrances

Main throne room

The same palace from outside

size of lakes. Palace buildings were made of brick and covered in white plaster. The walls were covered with colorful paintings. There were separate buildings for the pharaoh's wives.

Servants would have seen to all of Tut's needs. Each day they brought his food. Peasants ate bread and drank beer. But for a royal prince, there were meat and vegetables. Figs and dates. Wine was made from grapes grown in the north of Egypt, or from dates or figs or pomegranates.

It appears that young Tut was a member of "the clean plate club." A small statue of him reveals a chubby child with a plump belly and arms.

His servants also bathed and dressed him. They shaved his head, leaving only a braid of hair at the side. This was the hairstyle for a prince. While he

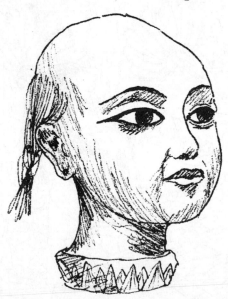

slept, they fanned him with ostrich-plume fans. That way, the heat would not disturb him.

Crocodiles lived in the Nile River. So guards kept watch every time Tut went swimming. Once he got older, he could ride his own chariot drawn by two fine horses with plumed headdresses. Or he

could sit back and enjoy a boat trip on the Nile.

Tut took his bow and arrow and went hunting with his hounds. In the desert, he might shoot an ostrich. Near the river there were ducks to hunt. Evidently Tut liked playing a popular board game called Senet. (He made sure four sets were put in his tomb.)

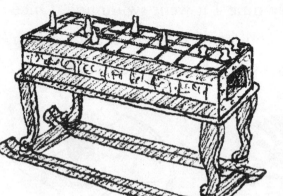

Did he like to play music? Perhaps so. Trumpets were found in his tomb. If he didn't want to play himself, musicians would play for him. They would play the harp and lute and pipe.

Because of the heat, even princes and princesses wore light, simple clothing.

Paintings of Tutankhamun show him in a pleated kilt of white linen.

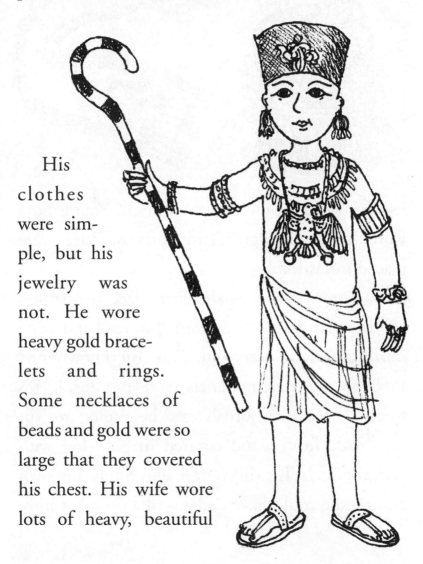

His clothes were simple, but his jewelry was not. He wore heavy gold bracelets and rings. Some necklaces of beads and gold were so large that they covered his chest. His wife wore lots of heavy, beautiful

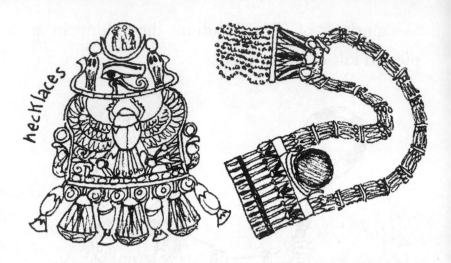

necklaces

jewelry. So did other royal children. Young boys wore heavy earrings. (Two pairs of Tut's were placed in his tomb.)

Ancient Egypt was the first place to develop a written language. Boys learned to read and write starting at four years old. Did Tut know how? Probably. Writing materials were put inside his tomb. A beautiful brush case belonging to Tut was made from wood covered in gold foil with gemstones. If Tut didn't feel like doing his own writing, he could have had a scribe do it for him.

A scribe's job was to write down all the pharaoh's orders and letters for him.

The Egyptians didn't have pens or pencils. Instead, they took a reed and chewed on the end of it. When the tip split apart, it could be used as a brush. Black ink was made from soot or charcoal. It came in a small, round block. A student had to dip the brush in a water pot before rubbing it on the ink.

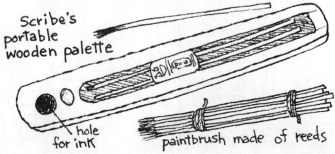

Scribe's portable wooden palette

hole for ink

paintbrush made of reeds

Egyptians made a kind of heavy paper, from papyrus plants along the banks of the Nile. (Our word "paper" comes from "papyrus.") The stem of the plant was cut into long strips. The strips then were placed in two layers, crossways, and pounded with a hammer. When all the juice was pounded out, the two layers formed a single sheet. That was put under a heavy stone until it dried out even more and became flatter. The last step was to rub the papyrus sheet back and forth with a stone until it was smooth.

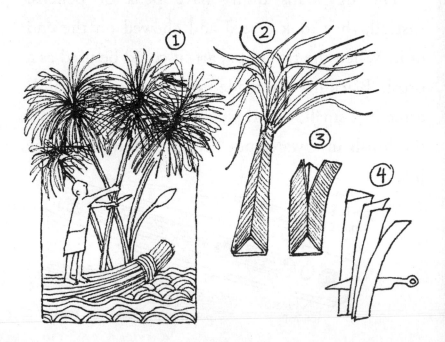

Instead of binding sheets of papyrus into books, the sheets were rolled up into scrolls. Papyrus paper was very strong. Some scrolls have been found that are thousands of years old. They are still in good shape. Papyrus was also easy to erase. A dab of water was all that was needed to get rid of a mistake.

As a child, Tut probably made lots of mistakes learning to write. Our alphabet has only twenty-six letters. His had about one thousand different

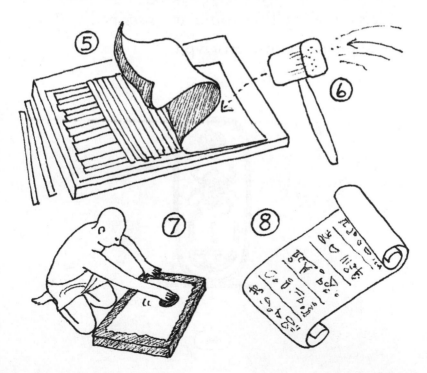

symbols called "hieroglyphs." Many hieroglyphs look more like pictures than letters.

After the ancient empire of Egypt came to an end, the meaning of hieroglyphs was lost for many centuries. No one could translate the writing. It was like a secret code that could not be broken.

Then, in 1822, a Frenchman named Jean-François Champollion finally figured out how to decipher (translate) hieroglyphs. Many of the objects in King Tut's tomb are inscribed with the pharaoh's name in hieroglyphs.

It looked like this:

HIEROGLYPHS

an alphabet:

A	B	C or Q	D	E or I	F or V	G
]	◿	◁	⬭	∮	⌁	⌂

H	J	K or X	L	M	N	O
🧬	〰	⬯	🐾	🦅	∿	⌒

P	R	S	T	V or W	Y	Z
▢	⬭	⎸	⌓	🦅	⫽⫽	≠

word pictures:

〰〰	➤	⏧	⋀
water	wood	metal	motion
⬭	◐	🦆	👁
mouth	nose/joy	goose	weep
♧	🧎	⊔⊔	🧎
face	man	desert	woman

THE ROSETTA STONE

IF IT WEREN'T FOR A LUCKY ACCIDENT,
THE MEANING OF HIEROGLYPHS MIGHT STILL
BE A MYSTERY. IN 1799 FRENCH SOLDIERS
FOUND A LARGE PIECE OF BLACK STONE,
CALLED "BASALT." THE STONE HAD CARVINGS
IN THREE DIFFERENT SCRIPTS: HIEROGLYPHS,
GREEK, AND A THIRD KIND CALLED "DEMOTIC."
THE WORDS ON THE STONE WERE WRITTEN
IN 196 B.C. TO PRAISE A PHARAOH NAMED
PTOLEMY V. ALL THREE LANGUAGES WERE
COMMONLY USED AT THE TIME SO THAT
WHOEVER SAW THE STONE COULD READ IT.

BY THE 1800S, NO ONE KNEW HOW TO READ
HIEROGLYPHS. BUT IF SOMEONE COULD MATCH
UP THE GREEK AND THE DEMOTIC TO THE
HIEROGLYPHS, THEY COULD CREATE A KEY TO
HIEROGLYPHS.

JEAN-FRANÇOIS CHAMPOLLION FINALLY
FIGURED OUT THE BASIC RULES OF
HIEROGLYPHS—AFTER STUDYING THE STONE
FOR FOURTEEN YEARS! FINALLY, AFTER
ALMOST FIFTEEN HUNDRED YEARS OF SILENCE,
THE LANGUAGE OF ANCIENT EGYPT COULD AT
LAST BE "HEARD."

THE STONE IS CALLED THE ROSETTA
STONE AFTER THE TOWN WHERE IT WAS
FOUND. TODAY IT IS IN THE BRITISH MUSEUM
IN LONDON.

Jean-François
Champollion

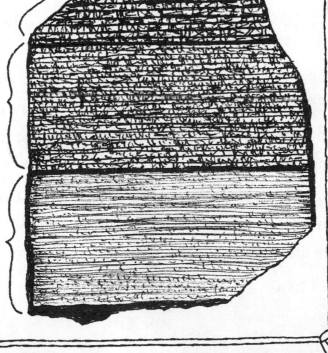

Hieroglyphs

Demotic

Greek

Chapter 4
An Early Death

During Amenhotep's sixteen-year-long rule, the empire did not run smoothly. The lands under Egypt's control had to pay tribute. This meant that every year they had to send riches to the pharaoh. For instance, from Nubia in the south came gold. Lebanon had to send rare cedar wood. But the Egyptian army had grown weaker. Tribute had stopped coming in.

Then Amenhotep IV was gone. And King Tut was just a child. How could he be expected to make the empire strong again?

The real power now lay with Tut's vizier, or chief minister, and one of the army generals. Tut was the ruler in name only. He appeared at important ceremonies and holidays.

If Tut had lived beyond his teen years, perhaps he would have grown up to become a strong and wise ruler. Or maybe he always would have been under the thumb of his advisers.

Perhaps they were afraid that if Tut had more power, he might try to bring back the strange ways of Amenhotep IV. Instead, the temples of the older gods were reopened. And Thebes, not Amarna, became the royal city once again. Tut moved back there with his queen. They may have had children. In Tut's tomb, along with his coffin, two tiny coffins were also found. They contained the bodies of two baby girls. It is possible that they were Tut's children.

King Tut and his wife

What we do know is this: He didn't leave a son behind to become pharaoh after his death. And even in a time when most people did not live to age forty, Tut still died very young. He was only eighteen or nineteen.

It is not surprising that some historians have suspected foul play. Perhaps the vizier or the general decided to get rid of Tut. (Each of them became pharaoh after Tut by marrying into the royal family.)

In modern times a popular notion was that Tut died from a blow to the head. But in 2005, CAT scans were done on the pharaoh's three-thousand-year-old body. Over two months, cross-sectional images were taken of Tut, from head to toe. (Think of Tut's body as a loaf of bread, with each image as a slice of bread.) When all the images were assembled, they created a three-dimensional picture of his body, inside and out.

So what did scientists learn?

There appeared to be an injury to his head, but it did not happen when he was alive. Tut's skull may have been injured when his mummy was found in 1922, so he was not killed by a blow to the head. However, the tests were not able to rule out all other methods of murder. For example, there was no way to tell if Tut had been poisoned. Evidence of poison wouldn't have shown up on the scans.

The scientists did find out that Tut had a broken leg. It is possible that this injury may have caused an infection that led to his death.

The tests on Tut are over now. His body probably does not need to be examined anymore. The man who headed the testing said, "We should leave

him in peace." Tut was placed in his coffin and returned to his burial chamber.

Chapter 5
The Afterlife

Of course, Tut had no way of knowing that he would die young. Nevertheless, he'd already started planning his tomb before his death.

Why?

The ancient Egyptians believed in an afterlife. Life after death was very much like life on Earth. In fact, it was even better!

The journey to the Land of the Dead was a difficult one. Not everyone was allowed to live there. A special book had magic spells that helped a person reach the Land of the Dead. The book was called *The Book of the Dead.*

THE BOOK OF THE DEAD

AFTER A PERSON DIED, HIS OR HER SPIRIT WANTED TO REACH THE LAND OF THE DEAD. A BOOK OF POWERFUL SPELLS AND SONGS WAS THOUGHT TO HELP THE SPIRIT ON THE JOURNEY. THE BOOK IS COMMONLY REFERRED TO AS "THE BOOK OF THE DEAD." OVER TIME, THE BOOK GREW LONGER UNTIL IT CONTAINED NEARLY TWO HUNDRED SPELLS. IT COULD BE PURCHASED BY ANYONE WHO COULD AFFORD IT. IT WAS OFTEN ILLUSTRATED IN COLOR, AND A COPY OF IT WAS PLACED INSIDE A COFFIN, IN A TOMB, OR SPELLS FROM IT WERE WRITTEN ON TOMB WALLS.

Osiris — A pool with trees around it — A Scribe — His wife

A papyrus showing people standing in their garden praising Osiris.

THE MOST IMPORTANT CHAPTER DESCRIBED THE RITUAL OF THE WEIGHING OF THE HEART.

The dead man   Anubis   The dead man's heart   The monster   The feather of truth

If the dead man had lied, the monster would eat his heart and he would not enter the afterlife.

Every person, even the pharaoh, had to pass a test. In the underworld, his or her heart was put on one side of a scale. On the other was a feather. If the person had led a good life, the heart would be lighter than the feather. And that meant the person could enter the Land of the Dead.

In the Land of the Dead, the person's spirit would continue to enjoy all the same pleasures as before. Eating. Drinking. Hunting. Playing games. Going for boat rides.

A tomb was not just a resting place for the body. It was like another home, filled with absolutely everything the person would need or want in the afterlife.

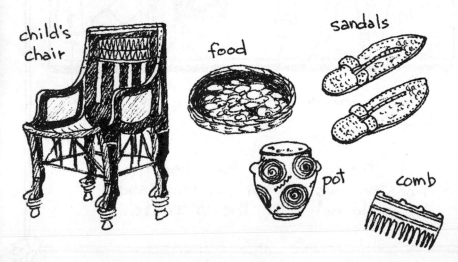

child's chair

food

sandals

pot

comb

Of course, poor peasants did not own many things. Nor could they afford large tombs. Often, poor people were just buried in the sand. But a royal tomb had many rooms, all of which were filled with treasures.

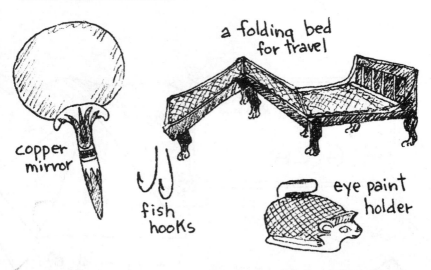

a folding bed for travel

copper mirror

fish hooks

eye paint holder

The tomb of Tutankhamun was very small for a pharaoh. It had only four rooms. That's because it was meant for someone else. Probably a member of the court. But when Tut died, his own much grander tomb was not ready. There was no choice except to bury him someplace else.

The largest tombs of pharaohs are the three pyramids at Giza. The huge statue of the Sphinx is there, too, watching over the pyramids.

The pyramids were built long before Tut's time—more than one thousand years before.

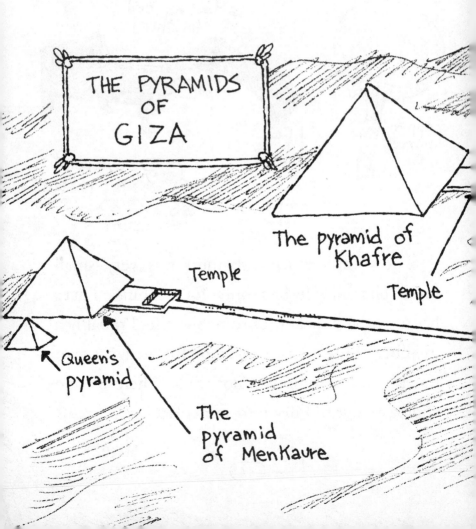

THE PYRAMIDS OF GIZA

The pyramid of Khafre

Temple

Temple

Queen's pyramid

The pyramid of Menkaure

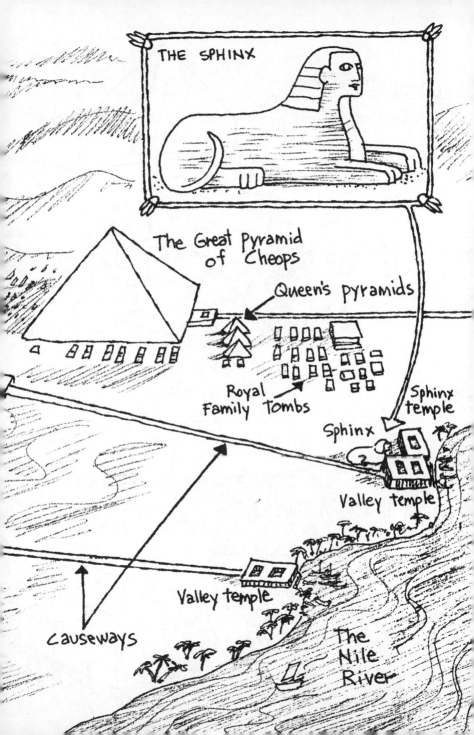

THE SPHINX

The Great Pyramid of Cheops

Queen's pyramids

Royal Family Tombs

Sphinx temple

Sphinx

Valley temple

Causeways

Valley temple

The Nile River

The biggest pyramid belonged to a pharaoh named Cheops. It took approximately one hundred thousand workers twenty years to complete. The body of Cheops was placed deep inside, in a secret chamber.

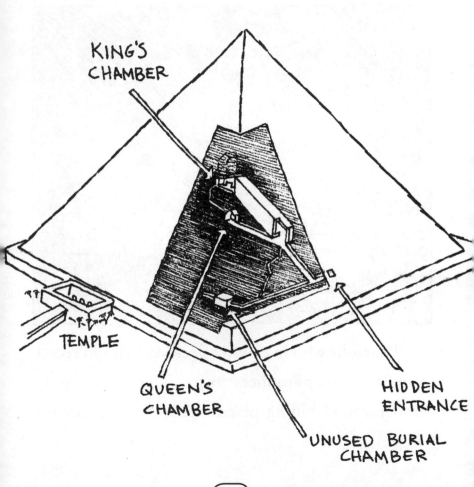

KING'S
CHAMBER

TEMPLE

QUEEN'S
CHAMBER

HIDDEN
ENTRANCE

UNUSED BURIAL
CHAMBER

In ancient times, people knew that treasure lay buried with the body of the pharaoh. Unfortunately, the pyramids were looted. Robbers made off with the objects meant for the pharaoh's afterlife.

Pharaohs who lived later decided to build secret tombs to keep robbers away. The tombs were underground hiding places. They had all sorts of traps.

Some tombs had stone blocks placed above the entrance. If the door was opened, the stone would fall and kill the robber. Inside, there were false rooms to confuse robbers. And if certain floor tiles were stepped on, they gave way, sending robbers down a shaft to their death.

But all the planning and all the traps did not stop thieves. Somehow they managed to find the tombs. They broke into them and made off with the riches.

Before Howard Carter found Tut's tomb in 1922, people thought every single tomb of a pharaoh had been opened and robbed. That was why Carter's discovery was such an important event. There always had been *legends* about the fabulous treasures of the pharaohs. Now there was proof.

The legends were true.

THE PYRAMIDS

THE PYRAMID SHAPE WAS VERY IMPORTANT TO THE ANCIENT EGYPTIANS. THEY BELIEVED THAT THE PHARAOH ASCENDED TO HEAVEN ON THE RAYS OF THE SUN. THE SHAPE OF THE PYRAMID WAS A SYMBOL FOR THE SUN'S RAYS, WHICH THE PHARAOH WOULD USE TO CLIMB TO THE AFTERLIFE. WHERE THE PYRAMID WAS PUT ALSO WAS VERY IMPORTANT. IT NEEDED TO BE UNDERNEATH THE MOST IMPORTANT STARS IN THE SKY.

THE FIRST PYRAMID WAS BUILT IN 2611 B.C. FOR A PHARAOH CALLED DJOSER. IT HAD SIX LEVELS THAT ROSE UP LIKE STEPS.

THE FIRST PYRAMID WITHOUT ANY STEPS, CALLED "THE BENT PYRAMID," WAS BUILT ABOUT THIRTY YEARS LATER BY ANOTHER PHARAOH. BUT IT DID NOT RISE VERY HIGH AND THE ANGLE BY WHICH IT WAS BUILT CHANGED DURING CONSTRUCTION MAKING IT LOOK "BENT."

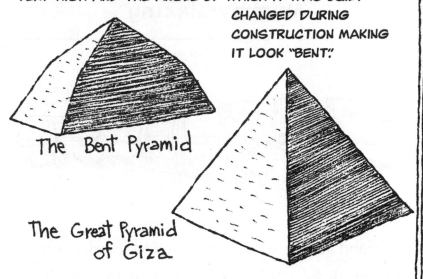

The Bent Pyramid

The Great Pyramid of Giza

FIFTY YEARS LATER, THE LARGEST OF THE THREE PYRAMIDS AT GIZA WAS BUILT. ABOUT TWO MILLION STONE BLOCKS, EACH ONE WEIGHING AS MUCH AS FIFTEEN TONS, WERE USED. ALTOGETHER IT TOOK MORE THAN EIGHTY YEARS TO BUILD ALL THREE PYRAMIDS!

FOR A LONG TIME IT WAS BELIEVED THAT SLAVES WERE FORCED TO BUILD THE PYRAMIDS. IN FACT, THE LABORERS WERE HIRED WORKERS. THERE WAS A LARGE VILLAGE NEAR THE BUILDING SITE, WHERE THE WORKERS LIVED WITH THEIR FAMILIES. THERE WAS EVEN A DOCTOR, IN CASE A WORKER GOT INJURED.

Chapter 6
Mummy-Making

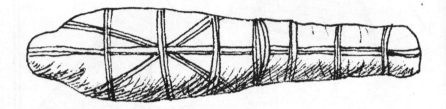

Food and furniture, clothes and jewelry. They would all be used and enjoyed in the afterlife. But the most important thing a person needed after death was his or her own body.

The belief was that the person's spirit returned again and again to its body. So the Egyptians learned how to preserve a dead body. They wanted to keep it from decaying. They wanted it to last for as long as possible.

What they did was dry out the dead body. They turned it into a mummy. Over the centuries the ancient Egyptians became better and better at making mummies.

Right after he died, Tut's body was ferried by boat across the Nile River. There, priests were waiting. Their job was to make his body into a mummy.

THE FUNERAL BARGE

From start to finish, it took about seventy days. First, the pharaoh's body had to be cut open. This was so the organs inside could be removed. The Egyptians believed that the heart was the seat of thought and wisdom. Tut's spirit would need his heart in the afterlife. So it stayed in his body.

But the priests removed his lungs, liver, stomach, and intestines. Each was put in a special jar, protected by a different god. Later on, these jars were placed inside Tut's tomb, along with his mummy.

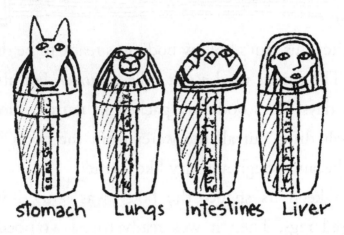

stomach   Lungs   Intestines   Liver

The Egyptians didn't think a person's brain did much of anything. So, with a thin hook that went in through the nose, they scraped out Tut's brain . . . then threw it away!

brain hook

Tut's body is drying in natron.

After this, Tut's hollow body was ready to be dried out. The priests used a salt called *natron*. For about forty days, Tut's body lay packed in natron. Slowly the salt dried out all the water from the body. The skin became tough and dry like leather.

To keep its shape, the body was stuffed with scented rags. Then it was ready to be wrapped in yards and yards of fine white cloth. The priests said prayers as they wrapped up the pharaoh's mummy. The wrapping took fifteen days. The priests placed little good-luck charms in between the layers of cloth.

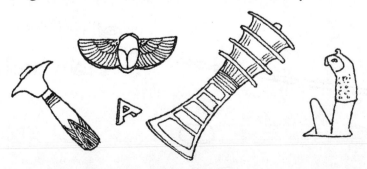

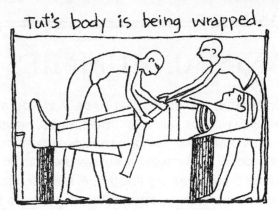

Tut's body is being wrapped.

Many of the charms were made of gold and pretty colored stones in different shapes. Some were heart-shaped. Some, called *scarabs*, looked like beetles. Still others looked like tiny eyes. They were meant to keep evil spirits away from Tut.

Once his body was all wrapped up, the cloth layers were coated with something like glue. When it dried, the wrapping became hard, like a shell around the mummy. Now Tut's mummy was ready for his funeral.

ANIMAL MUMMIES

BESIDES PEOPLE, THE EGYPTIANS MADE MUMMIES OF MANY DIFFERENT KINDS OF ANIMALS: DOGS, CATS, BIRDS, FISH, BABOONS—EVEN BULLS AND HIPPOPOTAMUSES! THEY DID THIS FOR MANY REASONS. SOMETIMES A MUMMY BIRD OR JOINT OF A COW WAS LEFT IN A TOMB AS FOOD FOR THE DEAD PERSON IN THE AFTERLIFE. SOMETIMES PEOPLE DIDN'T WANT TO LEAVE THEIR PETS BEHIND AFTER THEY DIED. SO THEY MADE MUMMIES OF THEIR CATS, DOGS, AND EVEN GAZELLES.

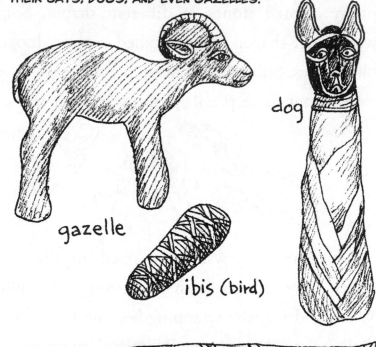

gazelle

ibis (bird)

dog

crocodile

THE EGYPTIANS BELIEVED THAT CERTAIN GODS AND GODDESSES COULD APPEAR AS ANIMALS. FOR INSTANCE, THE GODDESS BASTET SOMETIMES APPEARED AS A CAT. SO CATS WERE TURNED INTO MUMMIES TO HONOR HER. ONE TEMPLE TO BASTET HAD THOUSANDS OF CAT MUMMIES IN IT.

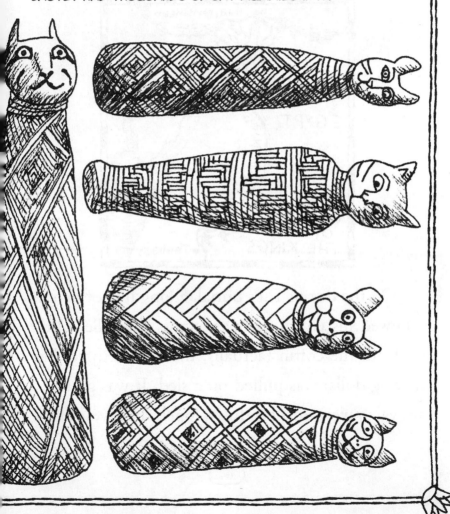

Chapter 7
Valley of the Kings

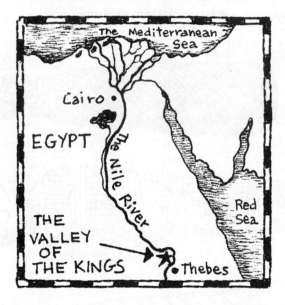

On the day of Tut's burial, a long line of people followed his coffin in boats across the Nile. Once on land, the coffin (actually, there were three, like nesting dolls) was pulled on a sled. It was going to a royal graveyard. This dusty, lonely area west of the

Nile was called the Valley of the Kings. In some photographs the area looks like a natural pyramid made of rock. Many other pharaohs were buried there, so priests stood guard, day and night. Nearby was a separate cemetery for queens and members of the court. It was called the Valley of the Queens.

At the head of the parade to the Valley of the Kings were the priests. Along the way they sang songs and chanted prayers. One of the priests wore a mask with a dog face on it. He was supposed to represent Anubis, the god of mummies.

Tut's young queen walked nearby. Following behind her were a group of women. They would have all been wailing and crying and tearing at their clothes. These mourners were there to express sadness over Tut's death.

After the mourners came servants, hundreds of them. They were carrying all the furniture, food, and other items to go in the tomb. They also

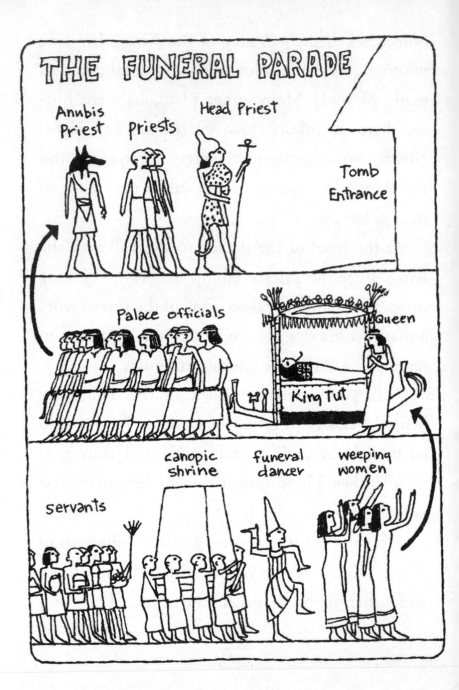

brought along many little statues that looked like servants. Once these were placed in the tomb, it was believed that the statues would come to life. Then the dead king would have all the servants he needed to take care of him.

Some of Tut's servant statues

At the entrance to the tomb, Tut's mummy was propped upright. The time had come for a very important ceremony. It was called "The Opening of the Mouth." While the prayer was said, a priest touched the eyes, mouth, and ears of the mummy. The magic was believed to bring the pharaoh back to life again. He would be able to speak and see and hear.

After that, the only thing left to do was to bury the pharaoh inside his tomb. Once Tut's mummy

was back in its coffins, it was placed inside a great stone box and hidden deep inside the tomb. A pile of rocks sealed up the entrance.

Afterward, all the mourners took part in a great feast. Everyone was joyful now for the dead king.

Tut was about to enter the Land of the Dead. He would live and be happy forever. They were sure that his mummy was safe, hidden away for all eternity.

But they were wrong.

Chapter 8
Mummy Mania

Ancient robbers were not the only ones who looted tombs in Egypt.

In the 1800s, people from many different countries in Europe began traveling to Egypt. The ancient kingdom was long gone. The old beliefs had all disappeared. The squiggly picture writing—hieroglyphs—was a mystery to everyone.

But tourists visited the Great Pyramids and the Sphinx. They took trips down the Nile River. They saw the ruins of old temples and giant statues. They wanted to bring back souvenirs. Sometimes what they brought back was a whole mummy! They might keep it in a room with other souvenirs they had bought. They might give it to a museum to exhibit. Or they might decide to unwrap the mummy and see what was inside.

"Unwrapping parties" were held. One English lord sent out printed cards for the party. His guests in London got to see "a mummy from Thebes unrolled at half past two." A German prince in

Berlin had a mummy unwrapped on his pool table. If a person couldn't afford a mummy all by himself, he could join a group. The group would pool their money and buy a mummy together. That's what a group of German people did. They each had a certificate. It was like owning shares of a mummy!

One man from Italy started a business of finding mummies to sell to customers. His name was Giovanni Belzoni. Sometimes he used a battering ram to get inside a tomb. He described an accident he had inside one. Feeling his way with a torch, he was looking for someplace to sit. What he landed on, with all his weight, were mummies. "I sank right down between broken mummies, a confusion of bones, rags, wooden boxes, which threw up such a lot of dust that for a quarter of an hour I was unable to move."

It is terrible to hear stories about the ancient dead being treated like this . . . just so someone could get rich quick. Of course, not all mummy hunters were in it for the money. Many people were interested in learning more about ancient Egypt, what life was like back then. People interested in finding objects that tell us about the past are called archaeologists.

THE END OF AN EMPIRE

DIFFERENT HISTORIANS GIVE DIFFERENT DATES FOR THE END OF THE GREAT KINGDOM OF ANCIENT EGYPT. SOME SAY THAT "ANCIENT EGYPT" WAS GONE BY 30 B.C. BY THIS TIME, THERE HAD BEEN MANY INVASIONS BY OTHER COUNTRIES.

SOME VERY FAMOUS "FOREIGNERS" RULED EGYPT AND BECAME PHARAOH. ALEXANDER THE GREAT TOOK EGYPT FROM THE PERSIANS. THE EGYPTIANS THOUGHT OF THE GREAT GREEK SOLDIER AS A HERO. AFTER ALEXANDER DIED, ONE OF HIS GENERALS, PTOLEMY I, TOOK OVER.

ALEXANDER THE GREAT

GENERAL PTOLEMY 1

CLEOPATRA

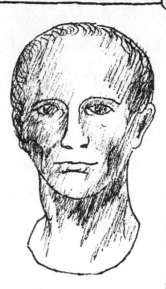

JULIUS CAESAR

PERHAPS YOU HAVE HEARD OF CLEOPATRA. SHE WAS A QUEEN OF EGYPT WHO LIVED FROM 69 TO 30 B.C. JULIUS CAESAR WAS EMPEROR OF THE ROMAN EMPIRE. THE ROMANS TOOK OVER EGYPT. CLEOPATRA THOUGHT THAT IF SHE HAD CAESAR'S CHILD, SHE WOULD HAVE MORE POWER. BUT IT DIDN'T WORK OUT THAT WAY. THE ROMANS STAYED IN POWER. WITHIN ONE HUNDRED YEARS, THE OLD EGYPTIAN WAY OF LIFE WAS VANISHING. HIEROGLYPHS HAD BECOME A "DEAD LANGUAGE." IT BECAME THE JOB OF ARCHAEOLOGISTS TO UNCOVER THE PAST.

By the late 1800s, many tombs of the pharaohs had been found. The trouble was that all of them were empty. The dream of every archaeologist was to find one that hadn't been looted. Many thought that was just a wild dream. They didn't believe there was even one tomb left with treasures. Howard Carter was practically the only man who thought there was.

Chapter 9
Howard Carter

Howard Carter was born in England in 1874. He was the son of an artist who made paintings of animals. Carter first went to Egypt when he was only seventeen years old. He was part of a group

exploring Amenhotep's city of Amarna. He drew pictures of the ruins. For a while, Carter also made money painting pictures of famous monuments to sell to tourists. Altogether he spent seventeen years living in Egypt.

The longer he was there, the more interested he became in archaeology. He grew certain that there was still an unopened tomb of a pharaoh. And he was determined to find it.

His search took place in the Valley of the Kings, which is on the western banks of the Nile near the modern city of Luxor.

The ancient tombs had been cut deep into the rock, with long hallways leading to the burial places.

It was going to take a lot of money and a large crew if Howard Carter hoped to uncover a hidden tomb.

At first, some Americans put up the money for a dig. (A *dig* is the name for this sort of exploration.) Then, in 1907, an English lord, Lord Carnarvon, agreed to help out Howard Carter.

LORD CARNARVON

HOWARD CARTER

Lord Carnarvon loved horses and cars. He first came to Egypt only because his doctors had told him to. He'd had an accident, and the hot, dry climate would be good for his health.

Once he was there, he became interested in the country's long history. When Howard Carter came to him, Lord Carnarvon gave him enough money to keep digging in the Valley of the Kings for many years.

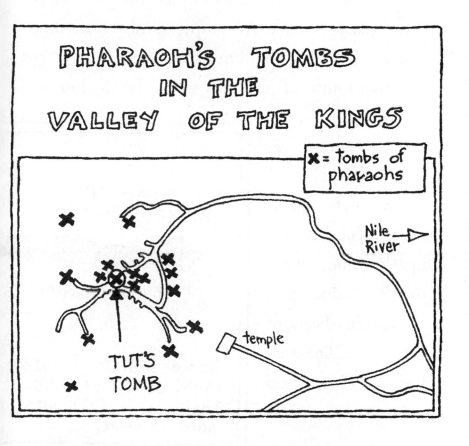

Howard Carter kept searching in one special area. He was sure Tut was buried there. He believed robbers had overlooked the tomb because it was in a low-lying part of the cemetery. A flood could have washed away all signs of the entrance.

But many other archaeologists thought it was a bad place to look. An empty tomb of another pharaoh had been found nearby. It seemed unlikely that two tombs of pharaohs would be so close to each other.

Still, Carter never lost faith that he was in the right place. Once, a cup turned up. Another time, the crew came upon some thin sheets of gold foil. They all had Tut's name on them in hieroglyphs.

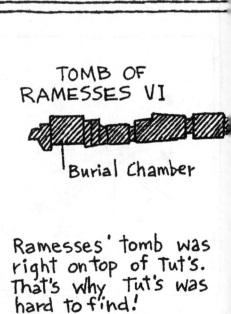

TOMB OF RAMESSES VI

Burial Chamber

Ramesses' tomb was right on top of Tut's. That's why Tut's was hard to find!

Year after year, Carter and his crew kept on digging. At one point they hit something. Something hard. Everyone got excited. But all they had found were workers' huts.

After that, Lord Carnarvon was ready to call it quits. How much longer could the search go on? But Howard Carter pleaded to continue the dig just

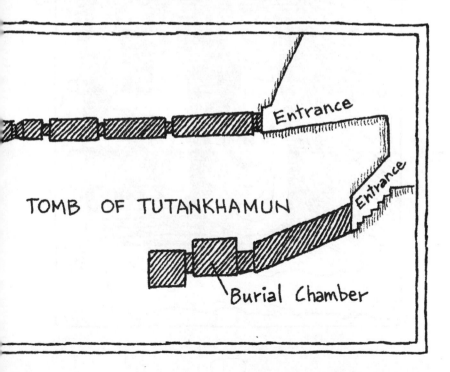

Entrance

Entrance

TOMB OF TUTANKHAMUN

Burial Chamber

for a little while longer. Maybe, just maybe, there was something else under the stone huts.

In November of 1922, the crew started digging again. After a few days they found a step. That may not seem like something very important. But

it was cut right into the rock. Pharaoh's tombs were cut into the rock, too.

Even more amazing, under that step was another step, and another. Howard and his crew unearthed a secret staircase leading to a door.

What was behind it?

What everyone in the crew wanted to do was open the door right then and there. But Howard Carter did not think that was fair. Lord Carnarvon deserved to be there, too. But Lord Carnarvon was far away in England. Howard Carter told the crew that they'd just have to wait for Lord Carnarvon to get there.

Of course, as soon as he learned the exciting news, Lord Carnarvon set out for Egypt. Today, it would take about five hours to fly from London to Cairo. Back then there were not many planes. So how long did it take him to finally reach Carter and his crew? Two weeks!

But at last Lord Carnarvon arrived. His daughter came, too. And Howard Carter was about to learn what was on the other side of the door.

LORD CARNARVON

LORD CARNARVON'S FULL NAME WAS GEORGE EDWARD STANHOPE MOLYNEUX HERBERT, FIFTH EARL OF CARNARVON—THAT'S A MOUTHFUL! BORN IN 1866, HE WAS AN ENGLISH ARISTOCRAT WHO HAD A LOT OF MONEY. AND HE SPONSORED CARTER'S DIG UNTIL TUT'S TOMB WAS FOUND IN 1922. ONLY A FEW MONTHS LATER, LORD CARNARVON DIED SUDDENLY. THE LIKELY CAUSE WAS AN INFECTED MOSQUITO BITE, BUT MANY PEOPLE BELIEVED THAT LORD CARNARVON WAS A VICTIM OF THE "CURSE OF TUTANKHAMUN." THEY WERE SURE THAT HE HAD DIED BECAUSE HE HAD DISTURBED THE PHARAOH'S TOMB. HIS DEATH LED TO MANY RUMORS OF OTHER "MUMMY CURSES."

Chapter 10
Gold Everywhere

When the stone door was opened, what lay beyond was a path full of rocks and pebbles. At the end was another door. Howard Carter knocked a hole in it. When he looked through, he held up a flickering candle in the darkness.

What did he see?

Here is how he described "the day of days, the most wonderful I have ever lived through":

"At first I could see nothing . . . but presently, as my eyes grew accustomed to the light, details of the room within emerged slowly from the mist,

strange animals, statues and gold—everywhere the glint of gold. . . . I was struck dumb with amazement."

Lord Carnarvon was there with his daughter. So was a friend of Carter's. They all were in the dark corridor. Lord Carnarvon called to Howard Carter, "Can you see anything?"

Howard Carter said, "Yes, wonderful things."

Howard Carter's dream had come true. He had found exactly what he was looking for: the tomb of King Tut.

What were some of the wonderful things he first saw?

There were two overturned chariots. A throne. Three big couches whose sides were carved in the shape of beasts. A bed with a linen mattress. There were life-size statues of kings. Things were piled

every which way. Vases and staffs of different shapes and sizes. One box was for the king's shaving equipment. Other boxes contained meat for Tut to eat.

And to the right of the jumble of treasure, Howard Carter saw another door. What did that mean? There were more rooms! There was more treasure!

This first room was the antechamber. The following day, Carter and Carnarvon and Carnarvon's daughter returned. They came with electric lamps this time. They wanted to get a better look around.

There was a hole in one wall. Peering through it, Carter could see into another room. It became known as the Annex. There was far more stuff in the Annex than in the antechamber. Smaller things like vases and game boards. And everything had been thrown about, all over the floor. Howard Carter realized that, long ago, robbers had definitely found their way in. But there was no way to tell what had been taken.

ANNEX TREASURES

wild goat

alabaster model boat

lion

All told there were four rooms in the tomb. This is how they were laid out:

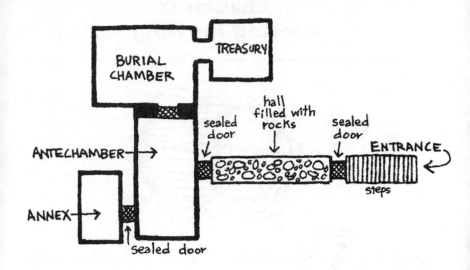

Another small room was called the Treasury. Among the things inside was the chest that contained jars with Tut's internal organs and the two small coffins with baby mummies. The most important room of all was the Burial Chamber. This was where Tut's mummy had been placed. But no one knew if the robbers had broken into the Burial Chamber, too.

Chapter 11
Meeting the King

King Tut was lucky. Until Howard Carter entered his burial chamber, his mummy had never been disturbed. For more than three thousand years, no one had laid eyes on it.

In the Burial Chamber, the first thing Carter saw was a gigantic gold cabinet. Inside of that was a great stone box. And inside of that was the outer mummy case. All three beautiful mummy cases fit together very tightly. The innermost one was solid gold—more than two hundred pounds of it.

THE MUMMY WITH THREE NESTING MUMMY CASES

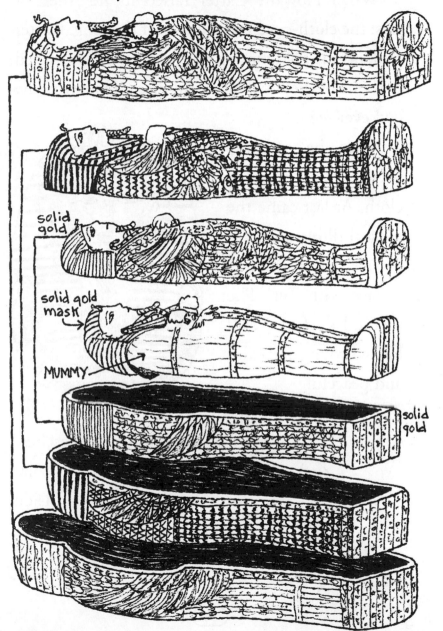

solid gold

solid gold mask →

MUMMY →

solid gold

When Howard Carter raised its lid, there it was: the cloth-covered mummy of the king. Carter took off the gold mask placed over it. He described it as one of the most beautiful pieces of artwork he had ever seen.

Then he carefully peeled away strips of cloth. At last came the most thrilling moment of all. He was face-to-face with Tut. The pharaoh's face still looked young and calm and peaceful.

Nearby was a chest made of white stone called *alabaster*. Inside were the jars holding the organs of the pharaoh. The ones the priests had removed from his body so long ago. Each jar had a stopper with a head of a god on it.

The treasures of Tut's tomb were sent to a museum in Cairo, Egypt. But Howard Carter did not send the king's mummy there. It stayed in the royal burial chamber, right where it belonged. That is where it remains now . . . in peace.

Chapter 12
The Legend Lives On

Right after Howard Carter's discovery of the tomb, scary stories started to be told. Stories about curses. Over the entrances of many ancient Egyptian tombs were warnings in hieroglyphs. People better stay away, the warnings said. Because anybody who dared to enter would pay for it.

Lord Carnarvon died only a few months after Tut's tomb was opened. A bad insect bite was the likely cause of his death. But many people were sure it was because of a curse. Tut was getting revenge. But if that were so, wouldn't Tut be angrier at Howard Carter? Yet Howard Carter lived until 1939 and died from natural causes.

For some people, stories of a curse add to the mystery of ancient Egypt. They like being scared. That's why horror movies about mummies are so popular.

Ancient Egypt was very different from our world. But it was a peaceful world. It was a world of great beauty. The people of ancient Egypt loved life so much, they hoped it would go on forever.

If people are lucky enough to see King Tut's precious belongings, that is what they should remember.

ANCIENT EGYPT'S LONG HISTORY

HISTORIANS DIVIDE ANCIENT EGYPT AND THE RULE OF THE PHARAOHS INTO TIME PERIODS CALLED KINGDOMS. THE OLD KINGDOM, WHICH STARTED IN 2575 B.C.–THAT'S MORE THAN 4,500 YEARS AGO—LASTED ABOUT FOUR HUNDRED YEARS. THE MIDDLE KINGDOM BEGAN IN 1975 B.C. AND CONTINUED FOR MORE THAN THREE HUNDRED YEARS. THE NEW KINGDOM DATED FROM 1539 B.C. TO 1075 B.C. KING TUT RULED DURING THE NEW KINGDOM.

BETWEEN THESE MAJOR PERIODS THERE WERE TIMES WHEN EGYPT WAS NOT AN ORGANIZED EMPIRE RULED BY ONE PHARAOH. HISTORIANS CALL THESE INTERMEDIATE PERIODS.

WITHIN THE KINGDOMS AND INTERMEDIATE PERIODS ARE DYNASTIES. DYNASTIES IDENTIFY WHEN A CERTAIN FAMILY WAS IN POWER. THERE WERE USUALLY MANY KINGS IN ONE DYNASTY. DURING THE NEW KINGDOM, KING TUT WAS THE TWELFTH KING OF THE EIGHTEENTH DYNASTY.

DURING THE LATE PERIOD (715-332 B.C.), EGYPT CAME UNDER THE RULE OF MANY DIFFERENT COUNTRIES AND LOST MUCH OF ITS POWER. THE LATE PERIOD WAS FOLLOWED BY THE GRECO-ROMAN PERIOD (332 B.C.-A.D. 395) AND FINALLY, IN 30 B.C., EGYPT BECAME A PROVINCE OF THE ROMAN EMPIRE. AN EGYPTIAN WOULD NOT BE KING AGAIN UNTIL MORE THAN 1,500 YEARS LATER, IN THE NINETEENTH CENTURY A.D.

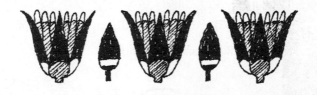

TIMELINE OF EGYPT AND THE LIFE OF KING TUTANKHAMUN

C. 5000 B.C.	Earliest Egyptian settlements form along the Nile River
3000 B.C.	Kingdoms of Upper and Lower Egypt unite
3100 B.C.	Earliest evidence of hieroglyphs
C. 2500 B.C.	The Great Sphinx at Giza is constructed
2600 B.C.	Construction starts on the pyramids of Giza
1550 B.C.	Construction begins on the temple of Karnak
1504 B.C.	Hatshepsut becomes the first woman pharaoh
1380 B.C.	The Temple of Luxor is built
1352 B.C.	King Amenhotep begins his rule
1343 B.C.	King Tut is born
1336 B.C.	Amenhotep dies; Tut becomes king
C. 1325 B.C.	King Tut dies at about age nineteen
1325 B.C.	The vizier becomes king after Tut's death
C. 1100 B.C.	Upper and Lower Egypt split
332 B.C.	Alexander the Great conquers Egypt
196 B.C.	The Rosetta stone's inscriptions are carved
30 B.C.	Egypt becomes part of the Roman empire
969 A.D.	Cairo is established as the capital of Egypt
1953 A.D.	Egypt is declared a republic

TIMELINE OF THE WORLD

Villages of mud-brick homes first spring up in Mesopotamia —	5000 B.C.
Pictographs used in Mesopotamia for record-keeping —	3500 B.C.
First wheeled vehicles are used —	3200 B.C.
The Bronze Age begins in Europe —	2000 B.C.
Builders begin to erect Stonehenge in Wales —	C. 1860 B.C.
First Babylonian kings rule —	1830 B.C.
Moses flees Egypt —	1487 B.C.
Iron Age begins in East Africa —	1400 B.C.
Construction on the Great Wall of China begins —	770 B.C.
First Olympic Games in Greece —	776 B.C.
The Great Wall of China is completed —	476 B.C.
The Parthenon is built in what is now Athens, Greece —	138 B.C.
Egypt is controlled by Byzantium —	395 A.D.
Egypt becomes Islamic —	641 A.D.
Jean-François Champollion translates the Rosetta stone —	1822 A.D.
Howard Carter is born in England —	1874 A.D.
Howard Carter discovers the tomb of King Tut —	1922 A.D.

BIBLIOGRAPHY

Barker, Henry. **Egyptian Gods and Goddesses.** Grosset & Dunlap, New York, 1999.

Chrisp, Peter. **Ancient Egypt Revealed.** DK Publishing, New York, 2002.

Donnelly, Judy. **Tut's Mummy: Lost . . . and Found.** Random House, New York, 1986.

Edwards, I. E. S. **Tutankhamun: His Tomb and Its Treasures.** Metropolitan Museum of Art / Random House, New York, 1976.

Glubock, Shirley, ed. **Discovering Tut-ankh-Amen's Tomb.** Macmillan, New York, 1968.

Hagen, Rose-Marie, and Rainer Hagen. **Egypt: People, Gods, Pharaohs.** Taschen, London, 2002.

Manley, Bill. **The Penguin Historical Atlas of Ancient Egypt.** Penguin, New York, 1996.

Milton, Joyce. **Hieroglyphs.** Grosset & Dunlap, New York, 2000.

Milton, Joyce. **Mummies.** Grosset & Dunlap, New York, 1996.

Ross, Stewart. **Ancient Egypt: Tales of the Dead.** DK Publishing, New York, 1997.

Silverman, David P. **Ancient Egypt.** Oxford University Press, New York, 2003.